BACKYARD BUGS

Louise Spilsbury

Crabtree Publishing Company

www.crabtreebooks.com

Author: Louise Spilsbury
Editors: Kathy Middleton
Crystal Sikkens
Project coordinator: Kathy Middleton
Production coordinator: Ken Wright
Prepress technicians: Ken Wright
Margaret Amy Salter

Picture Credits:
Dreamstime: Aprilleigh1352: page 14; Petr Malohlava:
page 16; David Mark: page 11; Sergeytoronto: page 5
Photolibrary: James Urbach: pages 3, 12–13
Shutterstock: cover; Alle: page 20; Joseph Calev: pages 1,
19; Anton Chernenko: page 9; Cre8tive Images: page 18;
David Good: page 8; Steve Heap: page 13 (top); Cathy
Keifer: page 15; Jakub Kozák: page 10; Tanya Mass:
page 7; Gherasim Rares: page 21 (top); Sapsiwai:
page 17; Ljupco Smokovski: page 21 (bottom); Marek R.
Swadzba: page 4; Yellowj: page 6

Every effort has been made to trace copyright holders and to obtain their permission for use of copyright material. The authors and publishers would be pleased to rectify any error or omission in future editions. All the Internet addresses given in this book were correct at the time of going to press. The author and publishers regret any inconvenience caused if addresses have changed or sites have ceased to exist, but can accept no responsibility for any such changes.

Library and Archives Canada Cataloguing in Publication

Spilsbury, Louise
Backyard bugs / Louise Spilsbury.

(Crabtree connections)
Includes index.
ISBN 978-0-7787-7841-7 (bound).--ISBN 978-0-7787-7863-9 (pbk.)

1. Insects--Juvenile literature. I. Title. II. Series: Crabtree connections

QL467.2.S67 2011   j595.7   C2011-900599-9

Library of Congress Cataloging-in-Publication Data

Spilsbury, Louise.
Backyard bugs / Louise Spilsbury.
p. cm. -- (Crabtree connections)
Includes index.
ISBN 978-0-7787-7863-9 (pbk. : alk. paper) -- ISBN 978-0-7787-7841-7
(reinforced library binding : alk. paper)
1. Insects--Juvenile literature. I. Title.
QL467.2.S698 2011
595.7--dc22

2011001333

Crabtree Publishing Company
www.crabtreebooks.com   1-800-387-7650

Printed in the U.S.A./072011/WO20110114

Published in Canada
Crabtree Publishing
616 Welland Ave.
St. Catharines, Ontario
L2M 5V6

Published in the United States
Crabtree Publishing
PMB 59051
350 Fifth Avenue, 59th Floor
New York, New York 10118

Contents

In Your Backyard

There are creepy crawlies all over your backyard!

Shapes and colors

Some bugs are long and thin. Others are round. Bugs come in different colors, too.

Aren't I pretty?

eye

Feel your way

Many bugs have **antennae** on their head. They use them to feel their way around.

antenna

Most bugs have huge eyes.

5

Ladybugs

Ladybugs are great climbers. They can climb up almost anything!

Don't eat me

Ladybugs taste bad. They are red or orange and black. Their colors warn birds not to eat them.

Ladybugs can walk upside-down.

spot

Count my spots!

Many ladybugs have seven black spots.

Hold on tight!

Centipedes

Centipedes are not fussy eaters. They eat any bugs they catch.

See me run

Centipedes have a lot of legs. They can even run backward.

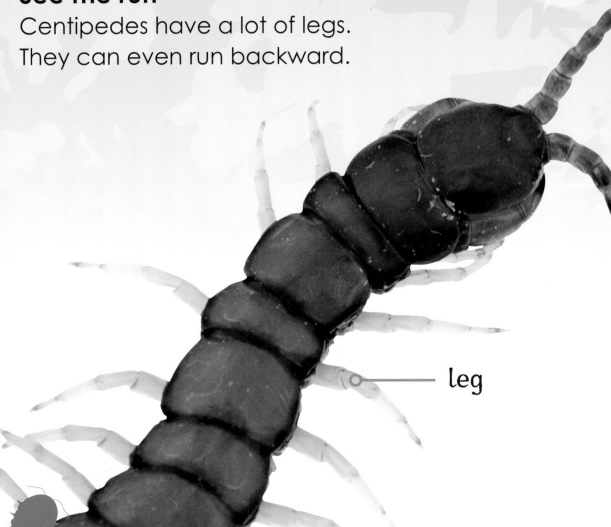

leg

8

Dinnertime

Centipedes catch food with their **claws**. They chew it in their **jaws**.

jaw

claw

Look at all those legs!

Can't catch me!

Grasshoppers

Grasshoppers have amazingly long back legs. They use them to jump.

Listen up!
Grasshoppers also use their legs to hear things. Their ears are in their knees.

knee

Many grasshoppers are green.

10

Talking legs

Grasshoppers make a noise by rubbing their legs and wings together.

Hop to it!

Shield Bugs

Shield bugs are the same color as leaves. This helps them hide from birds that eat them.

In hiding

In spring, shield bugs are green, like the leaves they eat.

Can you see me?

Smelly shield bugs are also called stink bugs!

Changing color

Shield bugs turn brown in autumn, like the leaves.

shield bug

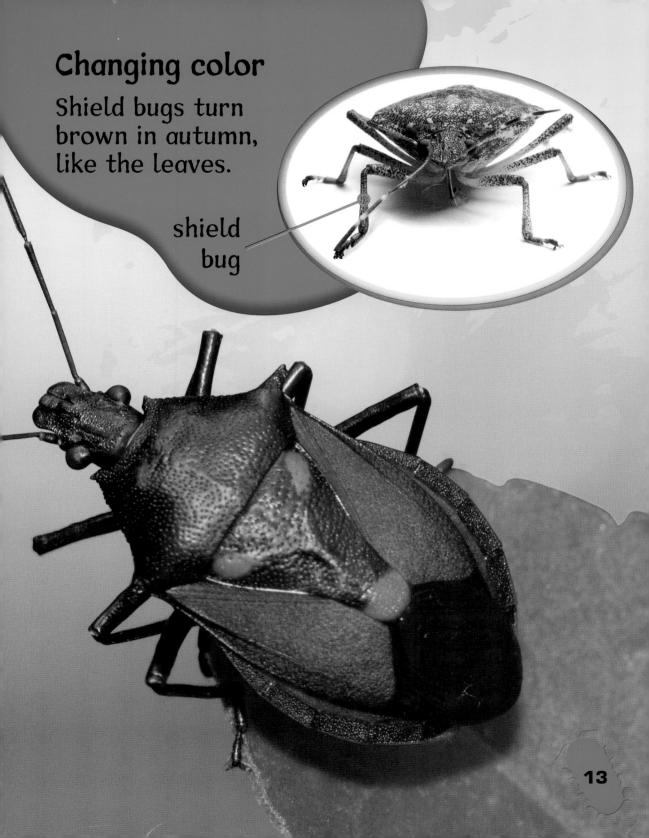

Spiders

Garden spiders have a good way of catching small **bugs** to eat. They make a **web** of sticky **silk**.

Sticky spot

Flying bugs get stuck on a spider's sticky web. Then the spider eats them.

Here comes dinner!

fly

Snack time

Spiders sometimes wrap flies in silk and save them to eat later.

My web is super-sticky!

15

Ants

Ants tell each other where food is. They leave a trail of smelly footprints from the food.

Follow that smell

Ants follow the smelly trail to the food. Then they carry it back to the nest.

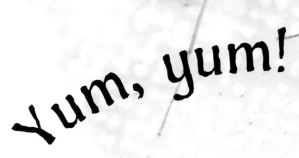

Yum, yum!

16

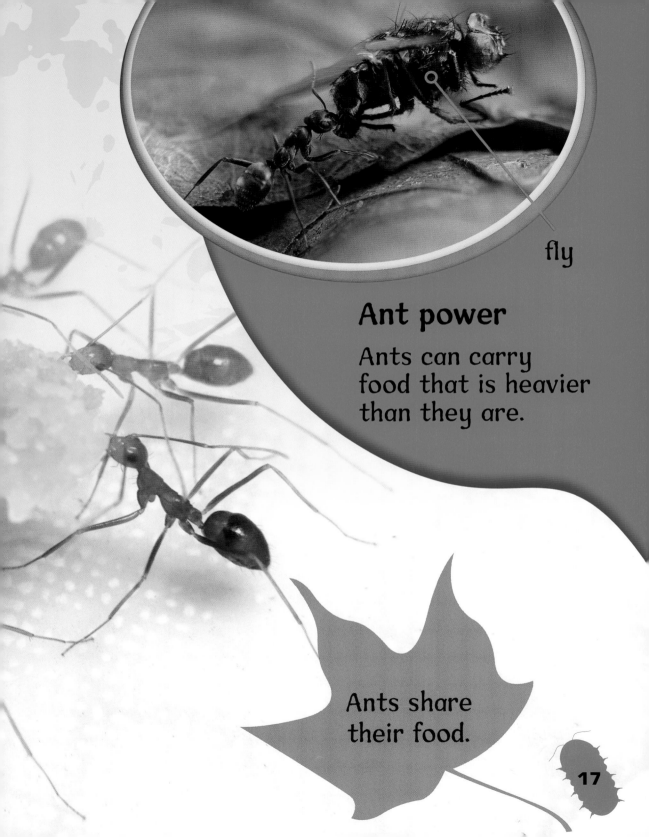

fly

Ant power

Ants can carry food that is heavier than they are.

Ants share their food.

17

Woodlice

Woodlice have super-tough **shells**. Some woodlice have shells that can bend, so they can curl up into a ball.

Drink up
Woodlice drink through their bottoms!

bottom

Woodlice use antennae to feel their way around.

So tough!

18

Roll up, roll up!

Some woodlice roll up into a ball if they are frightened.

antenna

Bees

Bees have strong wings.
They fly from flower
to flower.

Making honey

Flowers make a sweet juice
called **nectar**. Bees use nectar
to make honey.

Bees can fly a
long way.

20

Storing honey

Bees store honey inside their nest in cells.

cell

Buzz!

Glossary

antennae Two long thin parts on an animal's head. Bugs use antennae to feel and smell things.

cells Little spaces inside a bee's nest. Bees store honey inside these cells.

claws Sharp, curved parts of an animal's body. Animals use claws for catching and holding things.

jaws Mouth and sometimes teeth of an animal

nectar Juice found inside a flower. Bees use nectar to make honey.

shell Hard cover over part or all of an animal's body

silk Fine, soft thread made by spiders. Spiders use silk to make webs.

web A silk trap made by spiders to catch flies and other bugs

Further Reading

Web Sites

This Web site shows you how to make fun crafts of your favorite backyard bugs. Find it at:
www.dltk-kids.com/crafts/insects/crafts.htm

Find out more about the bugs and other animals in your backyard at:
www.backyardnature.net/animals.htm

Books

Living things in my back yard by Bobbie Kalman, Crabtree Publishing (2008).

The World of Insects series, Crabtree Publishing (2005-2006).

The ABCs of Insects by Bobbie Kalman, Crabtree Publishing (2009).

Backyard Encyclopedia by Rufus Bellamy, Crabtree Publishing (2011).

Backyard Bugs by Richard Ferguson, DK Publishing (2007).

Index